We can do no great things –
only small things with great love.

Mother Teresa (1910–1997)

My Thoughts with Love

A Grandparent's Keepsake Journal

ANNE GEDDES

To Mama,

My Thoughts with Love

from

Anna-Lynn

Date

ife itself is the most wonderful fairy tale.

Hans Christian Andersen (1805–1875)

*D*ate

Date ....

*H*appiness is as a butterfly which,
when pursued, is always beyond our grasp,
but which, if you will sit down quietly,
may alight upon you.

Nathaniel Hawthorne (1804–1864)

Date

Date

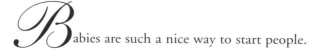

Babies are such a nice way to start people.

Don Herold (1889–1966)

Date

Date ....

Date ....

*D*o you believe in fairies?
… If you believe, clap your hands!

J. M. Barrie (1860–1937)

Date

Date

Date

*W*hat's in a name?
That which we call a rose
By any other name would smell as sweet.

William Shakespeare (1564–1616)

Date ....

Date

Angels can fly because they take themselves lightly.

G. K. Chesterton (1874–1936)

Date

Date ....

Date

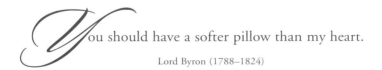You should have a softer pillow than my heart.

Lord Byron (1788–1824)

Date

Date

Date

Oh! little lock of golden hue,
In gently waving ringlet curl'd,
By the dear head on which you grew,
I would not lose you for a world.

Lord Byron (1788–1824)

Date

Date

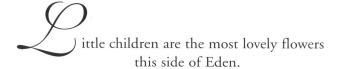

ittle children are the most lovely flowers
this side of Eden.

Rev. Dr. Davies

Date

Date

Date

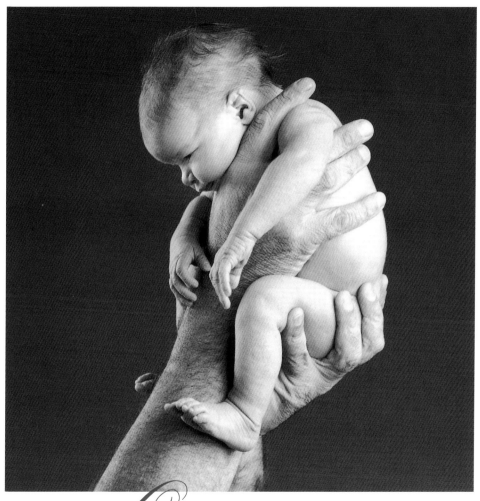

O wonderful, wonderful,
and most wonderful wonderful!
and yet again wonderful.

William Shakespeare (1564–1616)

Date

Date ....

Date ....

....

....

....

....

....

....

....

....

....

....

....

....

....

*T*hose who bring sunshine
to the lives of others
cannot keep it from themselves.

J. M. Barrie (1860–1937)

Date

Date

Date

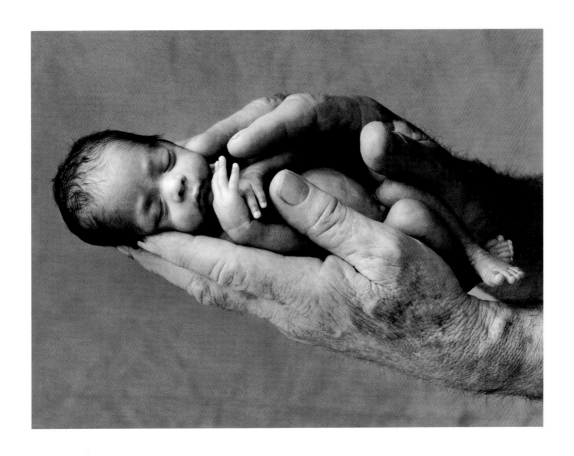

here are two ways to live your life.
One is as though nothing is a miracle.
The other is as though everything is a miracle.

Albert Einstein (1879–1955)

Date

Date

Date

*I*t lay upon its mother's breast, a thing
Bright as a dewdrop when it first descends
Or as the plumage of an angel's wing,
Where every tint of rainbow beauty blends.

Amelia Welby (1821–1852)

Date

Date

Date

The fragrance always stays in the hand
that gives the rose.

Hada Bejar

Date

Date

There are only two lasting bequests we can hope to give our children.
One of these is roots; the other, wings.

Cecilia Lasbury

Date

Date

The very pink of perfection.

Oliver Goldsmith (1728–1774)

ANNE GEDDES ™

ISBN 0-8362-1917-1

© Anne Geddes 1999

Published in 1999 by Photogenique Publishers
(a division of Hodder Moa Beckett)
Studio 3.16, Axis Building, 1 Cleveland Road, Parnell
Auckland, New Zealand

First Canadian edition published in 1999 by Andrews McMeel Publishing,
4520 Main Street, Kansas City, MO 64111-7701

Designed by Lucy Richardson
Produced by Kel Geddes
Color separations by MH Group

Printed by Midas Printing Limited, Hong Kong